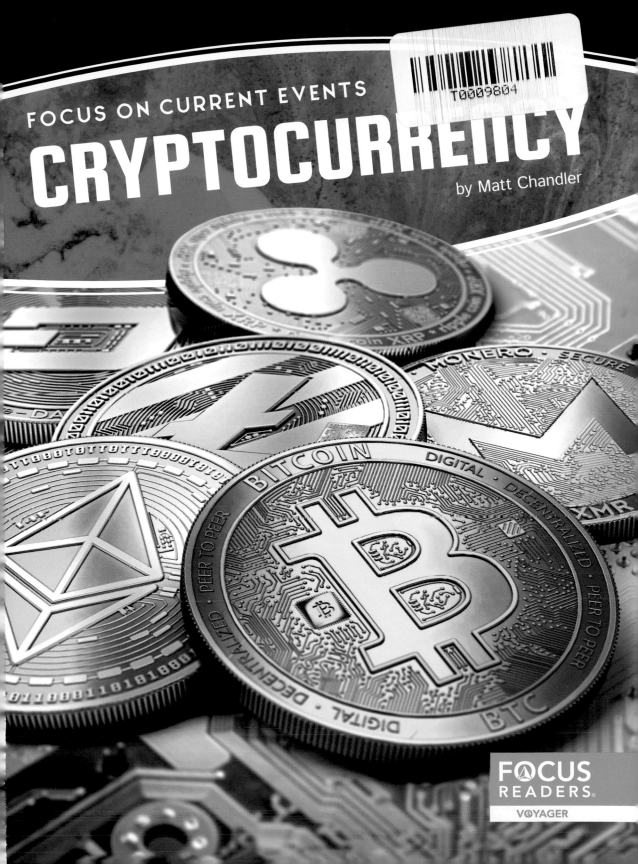

FOCUS ON CURRENT EVENTS
CRYPTOCURRENCY

by Matt Chandler

FOCUS READERS®

VOYAGER

www.focusreaders.com

Focus Readers is distributed by North Star Editions:
sales@northstareditions.com | 888-417-0195

Produced for Focus Readers by Red Line Editorial.

Content Consultant: Dr. David Yermack, Professor of Finance, New York University Stern School of Business

Photographs ©: Shutterstock Images, cover, 1, 4–5, 7, 11, 13, 14–15, 17, 20–21, 27, 28–29, 34–35, 37, 39, 40–41, 45; Horacio Villalobos/Corbis News/Getty Images, 8–9; Red Line Editorial, 19, 31; Ramon Espinosa/AP Images, 23; Chinatopix/AP Images, 24; Manuel Rueda/AP Images, 33; Koki Kataoka/Yomiuri Shimbun/AP Images, 43

Library of Congress Cataloging-in-Publication Data
Names: Chandler, Matt, author.
Title: Cryptocurrency / Matt Chandler.
Description: Lake Elmo, MN : Focus Readers, [2022] | Series: Focus on current events | Includes index. | Audience: Grades 4-6
Identifiers: LCCN 2021033819 (print) | LCCN 2021033820 (ebook) | ISBN 9781637390764 (hardcover) | ISBN 9781637391303 (paperback) | ISBN 9781637392317 (ebook pdf) | ISBN 9781637391846 (hosted ebook)
Subjects: LCSH: Cryptocurrencies--Juvenile literature. | Digital currency--Juvenile literature. | Bitcoin--Juvenile literature.
Classification: LCC HG1710.3 .C48 2022 (print) | LCC HG1710.3 (ebook) | DDC 332.4--dc23
LC record available at https://lccn.loc.gov/2021033819
LC ebook record available at https://lccn.loc.gov/2021033820

Printed in the United States of America
Mankato, MN
012022

ABOUT THE AUTHOR

Matt Chandler is the author of 75 books for children. His book *Side-by-Side Baseball Stars* was named Best Children's Book of 2015 by the American Society of Journalists and Authors (ASJA). Matt lives in New York with his wife and children.

TABLE OF CONTENTS

CHAPTER 1

MAKING HISTORY WITH PIZZA

Laszlo Hanyecz was hungry. He was also ready to make history. On May 22, 2010, Hanyecz used Bitcoin to pay for two pizzas. Bitcoin is a **digital** form of **currency**. However, at the time, it had never been used to buy anything. So, Hanyecz got creative. A few days earlier, he had posted a message in an online message board. He said he would pay 10,000 bitcoins to anyone who would deliver two pizzas to his home in Florida. The

By the late 2010s, various services allowed people to buy pizza with digital currency.

pizzas could be homemade. They could come from a restaurant. Hanyecz didn't care, as long as the pizzas were delivered.

Jeremy Sturdivant, a teenager in California, accepted the challenge. Sturdivant ordered two pizzas from a restaurant in Florida. He paid for them with a credit card, and he had them delivered to Hanyecz. In exchange for doing this, Hanyecz sent Sturdivant the 10,000 bitcoins. At the time, 10,000 bitcoins had a value of approximately $40. This **transaction** was the first purchase ever made using digital currency.

Since 2010, the value of Bitcoin has skyrocketed. The number of digital currencies has skyrocketed as well. By the early 2020s, there were thousands of them in use across the globe.

Digital currency is also called cryptocurrency. During the 2010s, cryptocurrency slowly started

hereum ▾

tecoin ▲ +1.2

itcoin ▲ +12.8 %

ipple ▼

△ May 22, 2021, marked the 11th anniversary of the first Bitcoin purchase. On that day, 10,000 bitcoins had a value of more than $370 million.

to gain wider acceptance. By the 2020s, people were buying it, selling it, collecting it, and using it to make purchases.

Hanyecz's historic purchase is celebrated every May 22 with Bitcoin Pizza Day. On that day, fans of cryptocurrency order pizza and celebrate the idea of buying goods with digital money.

CHAPTER 2

THE HISTORY OF CRYPTOCURRENCY

In 1982, David Chaum was a graduate student. At that time, digital banking was becoming more common. Chaum thought it was a threat to people's privacy. More and more banking information was available digitally. Chaum believed it would be easy for other people to see that information. He also believed criminals would be able to steal people's money more easily. So, Chaum created a digital program to protect

David Chaum discusses cryptocurrency at a technology conference in 2017.

people's banking information. He called his invention eCash. It was a cryptographic system of digital money. Cryptography is the process of changing a message into a secret code. When the message is **encrypted**, it cannot be understood by other people unless they know the code. The eCash system encrypted banking information. That way, the information would be secure when people made electronic transactions.

In 1995, Chaum started a company called DigiCash. His eCash system had created the security to send electronic payments. But DigiCash was the first company to actually use that system. In fact, DigiCash was accepting online electronic payments even before credit card companies such as Mastercard and Visa.

DigiCash was a huge breakthrough at the time. Even so, DigiCash was sending traditional

▲ Online shopping became common in the late 1990s, but digital currency did not exist yet.

currency such as US dollars and Mexican pesos. Cryptocurrency was still several years away from being invented.

In 2008, a paper was posted in an online message board. The paper outlined the idea of Bitcoin, the world's first cryptocurrency. The author was listed as Satoshi Nakamoto. However, Nakamoto was not the author's real name. No one knows for sure who invented Bitcoin.

The paper explained how Bitcoin would work and how it could change the way online business was done. Nakamoto described a form of money that was not controlled by any government or by the banking industry. Instead, Bitcoin would be run by a computer program. The program could not be interrupted or stopped.

Nakamoto believed this system would offer more security and privacy than banks. It would also eliminate the high fees that credit card companies charge for purchases. In addition, Nakamoto's system would not allow transactions to be reversed. Reversed transactions happen

➤ THINK ABOUT IT

Why do you think Satoshi Nakamoto didn't want anyone to know their real name?

One way banks make money is by charging fees. These fees can be expensive for consumers.

when buyers are unhappy with their purchases and they contact the bank to get their money back. In these situations, the sellers lose money. But with Bitcoin, transactions could not be reversed. As a result, sellers would be protected.

On January 3, 2009, Nakamoto put the idea into practice. Nakamoto created the first Bitcoin **block**. This event marked the beginning of cryptocurrency.

CHAPTER 3

WHAT IS CRYPTOCURRENCY?

When most people think of money, they usually imagine coins or paper bills. This form of money is physical. It exists in the real world. For example, suppose a woman walks into a store and wants a bottle of water. She gives money to the clerk, and the clerk gives her the drink. That is how transactions have worked for thousands of years.

People have been using coins since at least 600 BCE.

Now, thanks to cryptocurrency, people are using a form of money that is never held in anyone's hand. And it is not kept in a bank. Even so, it can be used to buy goods and services.

Cryptocurrency has three main characteristics. First, cryptocurrency only exists digitally. It is not a physical form of money like coins or bills. Second, cryptocurrency is decentralized. That means there is no government or bank that controls it. Instead, it is controlled by software. Third, cryptocurrency typically uses blockchain technology. This is a digital recording system. It is used to keep track of cryptocurrency transactions.

There are thousands of cryptocurrencies. They all operate using the same idea of a decentralized, digital system. However, each cryptocurrency has small differences that make it unique. Bitcoin is the oldest, most valuable, and best-known

Traditional money is controlled by central banks. For example, the US Federal Reserve Banks decide how many dollars are printed.

cryptocurrency. All other cryptocurrencies are known as altcoins.

One of the most famous altcoins is Dogecoin. This cryptocurrency began in 2013 as a joke between two software designers. Doge was a meme featuring a silly dog. But in 2021, Dogecoin went viral. It even caught the attention of billionaire Elon Musk. After Musk tweeted about Dogecoin, its price doubled. By mid-2021, it was one of the world's most valuable cryptocurrencies. Dogecoin demonstrated a basic principle of money. Something becomes valuable if everyone agrees that it is valuable.

Many people keep cryptocurrencies as an investment. An investment is when a person buys something with the hope that its value will increase over time. If the value goes up, the person can sell the item for more than she bought it for.

However, cryptocurrency can be a risky investment. That's because the price of cryptocurrency tends to rise and fall very quickly. For instance, an investor could buy $1,000 in

Bitcoin, and it might be worth only $500 a few months later. On the other hand, that same investor could buy $1,000 in Bitcoin, and its value might double in a few months.

BIG MONEY ◀

Bitcoin may get most of the attention, but there are several other cryptocurrencies with total values in the billions. This chart shows the top five cryptocurrencies on July 13, 2021.

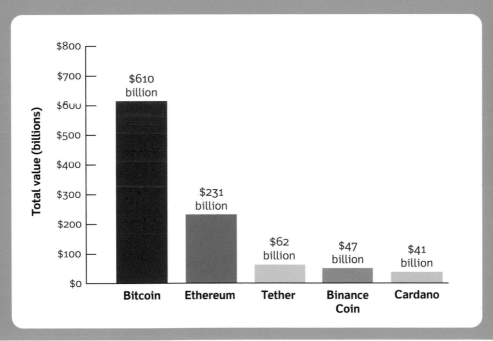

CHAPTER 4

HOW DIGITAL MONEY WORKS

ost cryptocurrency transactions take place on exchanges. These online platforms allow people to buy and sell digital money. However, before a person can buy or sell, she needs a digital wallet. A digital wallet is a software program. It tracks and stores the cryptocurrency that the person owns. Every digital wallet has its own address. This address is a string of random letters and numbers. It is similar to an email

Digital wallets can be created on cryptocurrency exchanges. Bitcoin ATMs can also create them on users' smartphones.

address. But instead of sending and receiving email, the user sends and receives cryptocurrency.

After the user creates a digital wallet, she can buy cryptocurrency on an exchange. To do so, she uses traditional money, such as US dollars. The cryptocurrency is then deposited into her digital wallet. Now she is ready to use it. For instance, she may want to send some of her cryptocurrency to a friend. Cryptocurrency is digital, so it is sent electronically. But the transaction has to be recorded. It also has to be verified. These processes are possible thanks to blockchain technology.

Blockchain technology is similar to a huge book of records. Every time someone buys or sells cryptocurrency, the transaction is recorded. These records are kept online and made public. Each transaction record is put in a sequence. The

▲ Digital wallets allow users to keep track of how much cryptocurrency they have.

records are also connected to one another using encryption. As a result, the transaction records cannot be changed.

The names of the people who made the transactions are not recorded. Instead, their digital wallet addresses are recorded. That means

▲ A cryptocurrency miner works in a room full of high-powered computers.

users can remain **anonymous** as long as no one finds out which digital wallets they own.

In addition to being recorded, every transaction also needs to be verified. But there is no bank to keep track of cryptocurrency transactions. Instead, blockchains rely on individuals. The process of verifying transactions is called mining. The people who do it are called miners. Miners group transactions together into blocks. A typical block can include 2,000 transactions.

The mining process prevents double-spending. Double-spending is not a problem with cash. If a person buys an item in a store, he gives money to the cashier. He can't use the same money at another store, because he doesn't have it anymore. Cryptocurrency miners make sure digital coins are not spent twice by the same user.

Miners earn cryptocurrency for their work. The mining process is so complex that people use computer programs to help. In the early days of cryptocurrency, miners could run these programs on their personal computers. But by the late 2010s, the process relied on large buildings full of specially built computers. In fact, Bitcoin mining uses more electricity than the entire country of Ireland does.

COINBASE

Coinbase is one of the world's most popular cryptocurrency exchanges. It was created in 2012. At first, the company handled only Bitcoin. But in 2016, Coinbase added the ability for users to buy and sell Ethereum, the second-largest cryptocurrency. By the early 2020s, Coinbase supported more than 60 digital currencies.

As of 2021, Coinbase had more than 50 million users around the world. Those users can buy, sell, and transfer cryptocurrency to other users. They can also convert one type of cryptocurrency to another. For instance, they can convert Bitcoin to Ethereum.

Coinbase is not the largest cryptocurrency exchange. However, many financial experts credit Coinbase with bringing cryptocurrency to the **mainstream**. One big reason is that Coinbase has followed the US government's regulations for

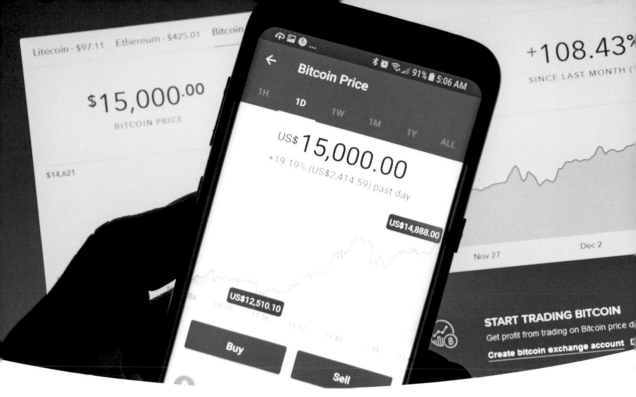

⚠ The Coinbase app enables users to buy and sell cryptocurrency on their smartphones.

money transfer services. As a result, the public gained confidence in the services Coinbase offers.

In contrast, other exchanges have not always had the confidence of mainstream users. For example, Mt. Gox was the biggest cryptocurrency exchange in the early 2010s. This service did not follow the US government's regulations. It also had problems with security, and large sums of bitcoins were stolen.

CHAPTER 5

ADVANTAGES OF CRYPTOCURRENCY

People may wonder why anyone would buy cryptocurrency. After all, its value tends to go up and down very quickly, making it risky. Even so, supporters of cryptocurrency point to several reasons to use or invest in it.

For sellers, using cryptocurrency can be cheaper than using traditional money. That's because traditional transactions often involve a middleman. A middleman is a person or company

In some cases, using a credit card can be more expensive than using cryptocurrency.

that helps complete the purchase. For example, suppose an artist sells a painting, and the buyer uses a credit card to pay for it. In this case, the middleman is the credit card company. The company charges a fee to the seller. It is usually around 2 percent of the purchase price. So, if the artist charged $1,000 for her painting, she would receive only $980. The other $20 would go to the credit card company.

Cryptocurrency transactions do not involve a middleman. However, they still involve fees. These fees go to the miners who verify the transactions. The fees are always changing. That's because they are based on how many people are making transactions at a given time. For instance, in May 2021, Bitcoin fees ranged from $7 to $23 per transaction. In cryptocurrency transactions, the person sending the money pays the fee. So, the person buying the painting would pay $1,000 plus the fee. The artist would receive the full $1,000.

Supporters of cryptocurrency also argue that it offers greater privacy than credit cards. With

THE RISE OF BITCOIN ◀

Bitcoin's value changed dramatically in its first decade of existence. This chart shows the highest value of one bitcoin in each year from 2010 to 2020.

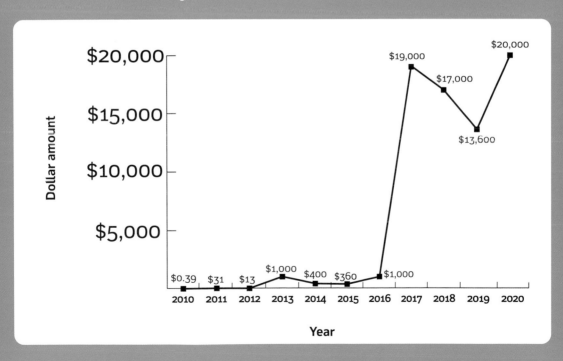

credit card purchases, **hackers** can get hold of people's names, addresses, and other sensitive information. This information can then be used to commit **identity theft**. In contrast, the blockchain is nearly impossible to hack. However, that doesn't mean cryptocurrency is perfectly safe. Hackers can still break into digital wallets.

Cryptocurrency could also help reduce inequality. Approximately 1.7 billion people in the world don't have a bank account. Not having a bank account can make certain transactions more difficult. Supporters of cryptocurrency say digital money could someday be an option for people who don't have easy access to banks.

Cryptocurrency supporters also point out that if a country's money system collapsed, digital money would survive. A collapse in the US dollar is very unlikely to happen, because the dollar is

Customers in Venezuela buy goods using Bitcoin in 2019.

relatively stable. However, Venezuela's official currency collapsed in the late 2010s. Some Venezuelans started using Bitcoin instead.

Even so, most cryptocurrencies could not work on a large scale. That's because most digital currencies use blockchain technology. There are a limited number of miners to verify transactions. As a result, it would not be possible for a whole country to switch to cryptocurrency. It would take too long to verify transactions.

CHAPTER 6

CRYPTOCURRENCY AND CRIME

Some people mistakenly believe that law enforcement cannot track purchases made with digital money. For this reason, cryptocurrency is sometimes used for illegal activities. These activities often happen on the dark web. The dark web is a series of websites where users can operate anonymously. People use the dark web for many legitimate reasons. But some people use it to buy and sell illegal goods.

People often use the dark web in countries where the government censors information, such as Iran (pictured) and China.

For example, Silk Road was a site that specialized in drugs and other illegal items. The site operated entirely with Bitcoin. The US government shut down Silk Road in 2013. However, it wasn't long before similar sites were created.

Cryptocurrency theft is another problem. In some cases, hackers have gained access to people's digital wallets. In 2019 and 2020, hackers stole more than $6.4 billion worth of cryptocurrency.

Despite these problems, crimes involving cryptocurrency are relatively rare. In 2020, illegal activity made up less than 1 percent of

➤ THINK ABOUT IT

Do you think cryptocurrency has more advantages or disadvantages? Why?

⚠ Most illegal transactions involve cash because it is nearly impossible to trace. But for online transactions, people may use cryptocurrency.

all cryptocurrency transactions. In fact, digital money is very risky for criminals. They may think they're anonymous because their names do not show up in the transaction details. But **forensics** companies can match criminals to their digital wallet addresses. When that happens, police are able to catch them.

DIGITAL MONEY IN THE MAINSTREAM

By the early 2020s, several major companies accepted cryptocurrency. They included Microsoft, Whole Foods, and Home Depot. Burger King and Pizza Hut also accepted digital currency in some countries. Coffee lovers could even buy Starbucks using Bitcoin.

However, there was still a long way to go before cryptocurrency was a common form of money. As of 2021, the vast majority of cryptocurrency was used for investing. Relatively few people used it to pay for goods and services. And most small businesses did not accept it. One big reason is that the value of cryptocurrency tends to rise and fall very quickly. For many small business owners, cryptocurrency isn't worth the risk.

▲ Bitcoin is accepted at some restaurants, but it was not a common form of payment as of 2021.

For example, suppose a restaurant accepts Bitcoin as payment for a sandwich. Today, the digital money may have a value of $10. Tomorrow, it might be worth only $8. Even if the restaurant sells the same number of sandwiches every day, the owner still can't predict how much money she's going to make. In contrast, the US dollar is a stable currency. Its value changes very little from day to day.

CHAPTER 7

THE FUTURE OF CRYPTOCURRENCY

By 2021, there were more than 10,000 different cryptocurrencies. Their total value topped $2 trillion. Owners of cryptocurrency have evolved, too. At first, they were mostly computer experts and tech people. Today, they include people from a wide variety of backgrounds. However, there is still uncertainty when it comes to cryptocurrency. The value continues to be unpredictable. And many financial experts see

Approximately 14 percent of US adults owned cryptocurrency as of 2021.

it as a risky investment. No one knows what the future holds for digital money. But people have a wide variety of opinions.

Mark Cuban is a billionaire investor. He is a strong supporter of cryptocurrency. Cuban predicts that digital money will eventually become common in the United States for two reasons. First, he says cryptocurrency will give people faster and easier access to their money. Second, it will lower the cost of transactions. Both, he says, could benefit low-income Americans.

But critics argue that cryptocurrency could end up hurting many people. In particular, it may lead to job losses. Some experts predict that banks will cut thousands of employees in response to the growth of cryptocurrency.

Supporters of cryptocurrency believe one of its major benefits is that it is not controlled by a

⚑ China's government-run cryptocurrency is known as digital yuan.

central bank or government. However, in 2020, the first government-run cryptocurrency was launched. The Bahamas, an island nation in the Caribbean, called its digital currency the sand dollar. That same year, China began testing its own digital currency. China's cryptocurrency does not use blockchain technology. For this reason, large numbers of people can use it. As of 2021, other major countries such as Japan and the United States were also looking into the idea of government-run cryptocurrency.

Cryptocurrencies run by governments are much easier for the authorities to keep track of. In theory, that would make it easier for law enforcement to stop illegal activities. However, many supporters of digital money oppose the idea of government-run cryptocurrency. They believe it goes against Satoshi Nakamoto's idea of a decentralized form of money.

Some countries have tried to slow the growth of cryptocurrency. For example, Turkey banned

➤ THINK ABOUT IT

Do you think governments should create their own cryptocurrencies? Why or why not?

In Turkey, some restaurants accepted cryptocurrency before it was banned in 2021.

digital money in 2021. Its government said cryptocurrency was too dangerous for citizens to invest in.

There are many questions about the future of digital currency. Still, there is little doubt that cryptocurrency has changed the way the world thinks about money.

FOCUS ON
CRYPTOCURRENCY

Write your answers on a separate piece of paper.

1. Write a paragraph explaining the main ideas of Chapter 4.

2. Do you think it's a good idea to invest in cryptocurrency? Why or why not?

3. When did the first purchase using Bitcoin take place?

    A. 1982
    B. 2010
    C. 2019

4. Why do many small businesses refuse to accept Bitcoin?

    A. They are afraid that the value of Bitcoin will change too often.
    B. They are afraid that Bitcoin will not exist in a few years.
    C. They are afraid that customers will not want to use Bitcoin.

Answer key on page 48.

GLOSSARY

anonymous
Unknown, or lacking an identity.

block
A file that permanently records a group of cryptocurrency transactions.

currency
A system of money that can be used to buy and sell goods and services.

digital
Having to do with information used on a computer.

encrypted
Put a message into a secret code so that it could not be understood by others.

forensics
The use of science to help solve crimes.

hackers
People who illegally gain access to information on computer systems.

identity theft
The act of stealing people's personal information, such as credit card numbers.

mainstream
The ideas or activities that are considered normal or commonplace.

transaction
An exchange of money, goods, or services.

TO LEARN MORE

BOOKS

January, Brendan. *Cryptocurrencies and the Blockchain Revolution: Bitcoin and Beyond.* Minneapolis: Lerner Publishing, 2021.

Kurtz, Kevin. *Cutting-Edge Blockchain and Bitcoin.* Minneapolis: Lerner Publishing, 2020.

Milton, Elizabeth. *The Future of Money: The Good, the Bad, the Bitcoin.* New York: Scholastic, 2019.

NOTE TO EDUCATORS

Visit **www.focusreaders.com** to find lesson plans, activities, links, and other resources related to this title.

INDEX

Answer Key: 1. Answers will vary; **2.** Answers will vary; **3.** B; **4.** A